T0198417

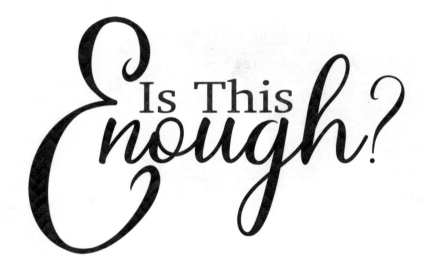

Is This Enough?

Written by: Libby Sandstrom

Illustrated by: Lauren Ballenger

WestBow Press books may be ordered through booksellers or by contacting:

WestBow Press
A Division of Thomas Nelson & Zondervan
1663 Liberty Drive
Bloomington, IN 47403
www.westbowpress.com
844-714-3454

ISBN: 978-1-6642-7806-6 (sc)
ISBN: 978-1-6642-7807-3 (e)

Library of Congress Control Number: 2022916878

Print information available on the last page.

WestBow Press rev. date: 09/13/2022

WESTBOW
PRESS®
A DIVISION OF THOMAS NELSON
& ZONDERVAN

For my dear granddaughters, Riley and Juliet, that they may know the many miracles of Jesus Christ.

It was truly a miracle you are about to read,

all the people were fed, and none left in need.

1

Jesus had been preaching all day and he needed to rest.

He had been so busy; it was for the best.

The disciples and Jesus climbed into a boat.

They rowed from the shore and began to float.

While he rested, five thousand men followed him along the shore.

All they wanted was to hear more!

Seeing the crowd, Jesus came to shore.
Having compassion, he healed the sick and poor.

All day long he preached.
So very many people he reached!

At the end of the day, the people stayed.

They stayed, and stayed, and would not go away!

That night everyone was hungry, and they started to pray.

The disciples wanted to send them away,
but Jesus instructed them to stay.

The people were all in a mass.
They divided by hundreds and sat on the grass.

A small boy approached with a basket of two
small fish and five loaves of bread.
"Is this enough?" he said.

The disciples looked at all the people,
and with their eyes opened wide,
"But you only have 5 loaves and 2 small fish," they cried!

Jesus looked to Heaven, blessed the fish and the bread.

The food was passed, and it seemed to last.
It lasted so long, that all were fed.

Twelve baskets remained of the fish and the bread!

Our offerings to God, be it your time, talents, or treasures, are never too small.
God can use them all!

You are never too young, or old, to serve the Lord.
Joy in this life will be your reward!

For further thought:

The feeding of the five thousand is found in the Bible after the story of the beheading of Jesus' cousin, John the Baptist. Jesus retreated to the boat for rest and prayer following the news of John's death. He needed to grieve, but he continued his ministry. When he came to shore he taught, and having compassion, healed the sick. Jesus has compassion for us and hurts when we hurt. The people interrupted Jesus' quiet time but, rather than view them as nuisances, he saw them as a reason for his ministry.

When the small boy presented the 5 loaves and 2 small fish it seemed as if there wasn't enough food for the five thousand men. It was likely more than five thousand people. Women and children ate separately and were counted separately from the men. It might have been as many as 10,000 people or more!

This miracle shows that if we give to God what may seem to be a small contribution, be it time, talent, or treasure, he can use it and multiply it. Jesus worked through the small boy to perform a miracle; we can never be too young or too old to be used by him.

For further reading

Matthew 14:15-21 NIV
Mark 6:35-44 NIV
Luke 9:12-17 NIV
John 6:5-14 NIV

Author Biography

Libby Sandstrom's personal mission statement:
"To ignite, nurture, and defend dignity in children of all ages."

Libby was born and raised in Ft. Wayne, Indiana. She has loved working with children her entire life. Starting at age 13, she began working with toddlers in Vacation Bible School and continues to be involved with VBS 40+ years later. In addition to teaching kindergarten level Sunday School for 5 years, she volunteered with a local program to Stop Child Abuse and Neglect (SCAN) for 3 years in Fort Wayne, Indiana.

When she, her husband Scott, and two children, Erik and Katherine, moved to Indianapolis, Indiana, in 1996, she began volunteering in Children's Ministries at Second Presbyterian Church. She has continued to volunteer in that ministry for 26 years. During that time, she was employed as Coordinator of Children's Ministries Volunteers for 5 years.

She also worked in school cafeterias for 10 years and co-founded the Nutrition Committee in her local, public school system.

She enjoys reading, writing, making greeting cards, watercolor painting, drawing, and crocheting.

Printed in the United States
by Baker & Taylor Publisher Services